A Tribute to
THE YOUNG AT HEART

LAURA INGALLS WILDER

By: Jill C. Wheeler

Published by Abdo & Daughters, 6535 Cecilia Circle, Edina, Minnesota 55439.

Library bound edition distributed by Rockbottom Books, Pentagon Tower, P.O. Box 36036, Minneapolis, Minnesota 55435.

Printed in the United States.

Cover Photo: Granger Collection
Inside Photos: Granger Collection 4, 8, 16, 19, 21, 26 & 32

Edited by Rosemary Wallner

LIBRARY OF CONGRESS CATALOGING-IN-PUBLICATION DATA
Wheeler, Jill C., 1964-
   Laura Ingalls Wilder / written by Jill Wheeler; [edited by Rosemary Wallner].
     p. cm.--(The Young at Heart)
   Summary: Discusses the life and works of the woman whose many moves with her family in her childhood provided the material to create her famous "Little House" books.
   ISBN 1-56239-115-1 (lib. bdg.)
   1.Wilder, Laura Ingalls, 1867-1957 -- Juvenile literature. 2. Authors, American -- 20th century -- Biography -- Juvenile literature. 3. Children's stories, American -- History and criticism -- Juvenile literature. 4. Frontier and pioneer life in literature -- Juvenile literature. [1. Wilder, Laura Ingalls, 1867-1957. 2. Authors, American.] I. Wallner, Rosemary, 1964- II. Title. III. Series: Wheeler, Jill C., 1964- Young at Heart.
PS3545.I342Z96 1992   813'.52--dc20   92-16568
                                              [B]

International Standard
Book Number:
1-56239-115-1

Library of Congress
Catalog Card Number:
92-16568

TABLE OF CONTENTS

Pioneers worked hard to build the railroads through the Dakota Territory.

PAINTING PICTURES WITH WORDS

In the spring of 1889, a twelve-year-old girl eagerly watched out the train window. She, her mother and three sisters were meeting their father. He had a new job working for the railroad in the Dakota Territory. (The Dakota Territory is now called North Dakota and South Dakota.)

The girl's heart pounded as she watched the country fly by outside her window. The train was much faster than the horse and buggy her family usually used. Excited, she turned to her older sister and described what she saw. Her sister, Mary, smiled as she gazed unseeing toward the window. A stroke had damaged the nerves in her eyes and she was blind.

The girl's name was Laura Ingalls. For many years, her eyes were Mary's eyes. Laura grew skilled at describing everything she saw. Her words made the sights of the Dakota Territory come alive for Mary. Laura painted beautiful pictures with words. Sometimes she grew frustrated because she could not find the right words to describe the wonderful sights she saw.

Laura saw many marvelous things growing up as a pioneer's daughter. She and her family traveled throughout the Midwest. They lived in log cabins and dugouts. They saw Native Americans and bears. They lived through winters so harsh the snow piled up as high as the roof.

Laura loved being a pioneer girl. She loved the openness and the beautiful prairie sunrises. As she grew older, she was sad to see how fast life changed. The open spaces she loved became crowded with people. Cars took over the roads. The wild animals left as more and more hunters stalked the open fields. All the while, Laura never forgot the wonders of her youth.

When she was sixty-three years old, Laura still had not forgotten. She wanted to share her special childhood with the world. She had been her sister's eyes. Now she would be the eyes for the world. Her memories would help a new generation experience the adventures, fears and joys of life as an American pioneer. She was ready to be the eyes to the world.

PIONEER GIRL

Laura was born on February 7, 1867, in the woods of Wisconsin. She was born into a nation still recovering from the Civil War. Many people were streaming into the unsettled land west of the Mississippi River. The people were called pioneers.

Laura's parents, Charles and Caroline, were pioneers, too. Both had been born in New York and moved to Wisconsin with their brothers and sisters. But Wisconsin wasn't far enough for Charles. He dreamed of the open prairies farther west.

When Laura was just one-and-a-half years old, her family moved to Missouri. A year later, Charles loaded up the family's covered wagon again and drove west to Independence, Kansas. He told Laura they were moving into a place called Indian Territory. Laura was excited – she wanted to see a Native American baby, called a papoose.

In Kansas, Charles built a log house in the country. Laura and Mary loved their new home. They picked wild flowers and watched the many animals and birds that lived around them. Charles killed some of the animals to use for food.

Pioneers lived in log houses.

8

He chopped down trees for firewood and to make furniture. The family found nearly everything they needed on the prairie. At night, their house rang out with the sounds of Charles's fiddle.

The Ingalls family was not completely alone though. They had a few neighbors. Once, the whole Ingalls family was sick with malaria. Luckily, a doctor happened to stop by to visit them. He gave them the medicine they needed to get better. A neighbor nursed them, too. Had it not been for the kind doctor and neighbor, the family would have died.

After a year, Charles received a letter. The man who had bought their house and land in Wisconsin did not want it anymore. He said he was leaving, and the Ingalls family could have their land back. Soon Charles, Caroline, Mary, Laura and their new baby sister, Carrie, were on their way back to the Wisconsin woods.

A WANDERING WE WILL GO

Laura was only four years old when her family returned to Wisconsin. It was the first of many moves they would make over the years. Charles loved to travel. He managed to find work wherever they went. Sometimes he worked as a carpenter. Sometimes he farmed. He took whatever jobs he could to feed and clothe his family.

Soon after they returned to Wisconsin, Mary and Laura began school. Laura was not fond of school. She would rather run outside and play than sit in a school and learn how to be a little lady. But her mother insisted. Her mother had been a schoolteacher before she married Laura's father.

The Ingalls family shared many happy times during their years in Wisconsin. There were games with cousins, brushes with wild fires and neighborhood parties. Laura remembered many of these events clearly even though she was very young when they happened.

When Laura was six, the family moved again. Charles felt there were too many people in Wisconsin. The people were scaring away the wild animals he hunted for food.

He wanted to go west. He sold the land and once again their covered wagon creaked across the woods.

The family stopped in the country near Walnut Grove, Minnesota. Charles traded his wagon for a house. They almost couldn't find the house – it was dug into the side of a creek bank. Laura was disappointed they had stopped traveling. She liked seeing new places. Over time she grew to like their new home on Plum Creek.

A CLOUD OF DESTRUCTION

The winter passed, and in the spring Charles built a new house on the other side of the creek. Mary and Laura began school in Walnut Grove. They attended church in town every Sunday, too. During the week, Charles tended his wheat field. It looked like it would be a bumper crop.

Everything changed one day when a strange cloud nearly covered the sun. The cloud was made of thousands of grasshoppers. The grasshoppers dropped from the sky and ate everything in sight – including the wheat field.

With no crop to sell, Laura's father left home to work on other people's farms.

When he returned, the family moved to town. Caroline was going to have another baby and Charles wanted her to be close to a doctor. The baby came in November 1875. It was a boy. Charles and Caroline called him Freddie.

The next year, the eggs the grasshoppers had laid the year before hatched. The new grasshoppers ate all the crops. Charles and Caroline decided to move once more. They traveled to southeastern Minnesota where Laura's Uncle Peter lived. While they were visiting there, baby Freddie died.

The family was very sad, but they had to move on. Charles found a job running a hotel in nearby Burr Oak, Iowa. Mary and Laura helped their parents run the hotel. They also went back to school. When the hotel's owners sold it, Charles took other jobs and the family moved two more times. Caroline also had another baby in May 1877. They named their new daughter Grace.

The Ingalls had been in Burr Oak less than a year when Charles decided to move again. He did not like Burr Oak.

Once more, he longed to go west. In the fall of 1877, the Ingalls family returned to Walnut Grove. Charles worked at a hotel there, then set up a butcher shop. He made enough money to build the family another house in town. Laura was glad to be back in Walnut Grove. She saw her old friends again at school and in church.

Even though Laura was only ten years old, she took odd jobs to help her family. She babysat and helped other people with chores. Sometimes she even went to live with other people to help them. It made her very homesick.

Laura forgot about being homesick when Mary became very ill in 1879. Mary's fever caused her to have a stroke. The stroke made her blind. Suddenly, Laura had to take care of Mary as well as her two younger sisters.

GO WEST!

Then one day, Charles heard there were jobs on the railroad out in Dakota Territory. It didn't take long for him to decide what he wanted to do. He moved to the town of DeSmet in what is now South Dakota. Soon after, Caroline, Mary, Laura, Carrie and Grace met him there. Laura had begun a new chapter in her life.

There were only a handful of people in DeSmet when the Ingalls family arrived. That changed quickly when the railroad began operating. The tiny town on the prairie came alive with new residents. Some of these people were homesteaders. They could own a section of land, or homestead, if they lived on it and farmed it for several years.

When Charles completed his railway job, he became a homesteader, too. He built the family a house on the homestead and a house in town. They lived in the town house in the winter.

One winter was the worst anyone could remember. It snowed so much the snow piled up almost to the roofs of the houses. The trains could not come through with supplies.

Near the end of the winter, the settlers ran out of food. A brave young man named Almanzo Wilder saved the day. He and a friend risked their lives to travel to another town and buy wheat for the settlers to make into bread.

FROM STUDENT TO TEACHER

Once again, Laura went back to school. She had a mission now – she was going to be a school teacher. She wanted to make enough money to help send Mary to a special school for the blind. Laura was very proud the day Mary left for the school. She also felt a little lonely. She would catch herself thinking how to describe something to Mary. Then she would remember Mary was gone.

Laura found other ways to keep busy after Mary left. There was church, school and parties with singing and charades. At a party one night, Almanzo Wilder asked Laura if he could walk her home. Laura wasn't sure what to do. She agreed, but they barely spoke to each other. Later, Laura learned one of Almanzo's friends had dared him to ask to walk a girl home.

Laura Ingalls Wilder taught in a small school house like the one above.

The friend had meant the woman who was standing behind Laura at the party. Almanzo mistakenly thought he meant Laura.

Laura began spending more and more time with Almanzo. One winter when she was just fifteen, she took a job teaching at a nearby school. She was lonely living away from home. She was glad when Almanzo picked her up in his sleigh to take her home every weekend.

When spring came and Laura finished teaching, she helped Almanzo break in a new team of horses. The two continued to see each other for two more years. During that time, Laura taught in several other schools. She also took odd jobs helping sew. She saved all the money she earned to help pay for Mary's school.

When Laura was eighteen, she and Almanzo were married. They moved to a small house Almanzo had built for them near DeSmet. Laura had changed from a pioneer girl to a farmer's wife.

MARRIED LIFE

Laura was no stranger to hardship. She saw her father's crops destroyed in hours. She watched her baby brother die. She moved from town to town. Her first years of married life proved no different.

It was a tough time to be farming on the Dakota prairie. Farmers hopefully planted seeds only to watch the hot sun bake and shrivel their crops. Other times hailstorms rushed across the prairie without warning and destroyed the crops. "There were dry years in the Dakotas when we were beginning our life together," Laura remembered. "How heart breaking it was to watch the grain we had sown with such high hopes wither and yellow in the hot winds."

Laura and Almanzo barely made enough money to pay their bills. Their uncertain future even overshadowed the birth of their daughter, Rose, in December 1886. The following summer, their barn burned to the ground. The next spring, Laura and Almanzo became very ill. The disease gave Almanzo a limp for the rest of his life.

Laura and Almanzo Wilder

In the summer of 1889, Laura and Almanzo had a baby boy. Twelve days later, the baby died. Two weeks after that a fire destroyed their house. The only thing Laura saved from the fire was a glass bread plate. The plate had been their first Christmas gift to each other.

By the next spring, Laura and Almanzo admitted defeat. They loaded up their few belongings and headed south to Florida. They lived there two years, but Laura hated the hot, damp climate. She wanted to leave, but she didn't know where to go. Finally, she and Almanzo decided to move back to DeSmet. There was no where else to go.

STARTING OVER

Laura's homecoming was not happy. Painful thoughts of her first years of marriage had replaced the joyful memories of her youth. With little money, she took a job sewing and Almanzo did whatever odd jobs he could find. They saved their money to move again.

Many pioneers struggled over the plains in long wagon trains.

In summer 1894, they decided to leave for Missouri. Laura wanted to live where the winters were mild. Almanzo heard the land in Missouri was good for farming. He was disappointed when they arrived and found the land rocky, hilly and covered with brush. They looked at a farm that had nothing but a little log house.

"The place looked unpromising enough when we first saw it," Almanzo said. "Coming from such a smooth country the place looked so rough to me that I hesitated to buy it. But wife had taken a violent fancy to this particular piece of land, saying if she could not have it she did not want any because it could be made into such a pretty place."

Laura's heart won, and they bought the land. They named it Rocky Ridge Farm. Laura loved the little house and farm. It reminded her of the many little houses she had lived in as a girl.

FARM WIFE

Slowly, Rocky Ridge Farm took shape. Laura and Almanzo put in many hours of hard work. They cleared land and planted apple trees. They raised sheep, cows, chickens, hogs and goats. Laura raised fruits and vegetables to sell. She also helped Almanzo saw wood to sell. Rose started school in nearby Mansfield, Missouri.

As the farm prospered, Laura and Almanzo turned their attention to the house. Almanzo built a small frame house next to the log house. Over the years, he added rooms. Laura wanted the house built of materials from their farm. She also wanted many windows. She wanted to look out on the land like she had as a child in her parents' covered wagon.

With the farm running smoothly, Laura turned her attention to other activities. She organized clubs so the local women could get together and discuss topics other than farming. She also began writing articles for local newspapers. She submitted columns for the *State Farmer*, both of the newspapers in St. Louis and the *Missouri Ruralist* newspaper.

COUNTRY JOURNALIST

Laura wrote about what her neighbors were doing. She wrote about the joys of the simple life and her experiences as a pioneer girl. For a while, she wrote a regular column on farm life called "The Farm Home." Later, she wrote a column called "As a Farm Woman Thinks." Her writings reflected her rural childhood as well as her talent for vivid description. She helped readers see her thoughts as she'd helped her sister see the beauty of the Dakota prairie. Words were important to her.

"The use of words is of itself an interesting study," she said. "You will hardly believe the difference the use of one word rather than another will make until you begin to hunt for a word with just the right shade of meaning, just the right color for the picture you are painting with words."

Laura's father's death in 1902 dimmed her happiness. She made it to DeSmet to see him before he died. Afterwards, she felt more lonely than ever. She had been like her father in many ways.

A TRIP TO THE WEST

The loneliness came again when Rose went off to college. Laura and Almanzo missed her, but they took pride in her accomplishments. She became a famous writer and newspaper reporter. She traveled around the world. For a while, she lived and worked in San Francisco. Time after time, Rose begged Laura to come visit her and her husband, Gillette Lane. Finally, in the summer of 1915, Laura agreed.

Laura was forty-eight years old when she visited San Francisco. She marveled at the Golden Gate Bridge, Chinatown and the thousands of people. She wrote many letters to Almanzo describing all she saw. She also admitted she missed Rocky Ridge Farm.

"Honest fact, I'm homesick," she wrote to him. "But there are so many interesting things still to be seen and I am here, that I feel I must see some more of them before I leave. Then I do want to do a little writing with Rose to get the hang of it a little better so I can write something that perhaps I can sell."

Laura Ingalls Wilder

A little later in the letter she summed up her feelings about the bustling city by the bay. "Believe me, there is no place like the country to live and I have not heard of anything so far that would lead me to give up Rocky Ridge for any other place," she wrote.

Laura did not wish to follow in her daughter's footsteps by living in the city. She did follow her in her choice of a writing career. While in San Francisco, Laura wrote an article on the Panama Pacific International Exposition, which was going on in the city at the time. Her articles appeared in the *Missouri Ruralist* and the *St. Louis Post Dispatch*. She resumed her writing when she returned to Rocky Ridge in fall 1915.

LITTLE HOUSE IN THE BIG WOODS

Laura slowed her writing pace after her mother and Mary died in 1924. She also took a break from the women's clubs and civic organizations to which she belonged. Together with Almanzo, she began selling parts of Rocky Ridge Farm. Her mother and sister's deaths had made her realize how time changes everything.

Many times she found her mind wandering back to the days of her childhood. She heard her father's fiddle and saw the waving grasses and flowers of the unspoiled prairie. She knew those days were gone, but she did not want people to forget them. Rose urged her to write down her memories to make sure they would survive.

One day in 1930 when Laura was sixty-three years old, she took her daughter's advice. She sat down at the small wooden desk on the farm she and Almanzo had carved out of the wilderness and began to write. Her pencil scratched across the tablet, bringing her father and mother, her friends, and the untamed west back to life.

"When I began writing children's stories, I had in mind only one book," she said. "For years I had thought that the stories my father told me should be passed on to other children. I felt they were much too good to be lost. And so I wrote the *Little House in the Big Woods*."

Little House in the Big Woods was published two years later. It was an instant hit. Thousands of people bought it and enjoyed its warm tales of pioneer life. Many began clamoring for more, much to Laura's surprise.

"I thought that would end it, but what do you think?" Laura said. "Children who read it wrote to me begging for more. I was amazed because I didn't know how to write. I went to little red schoolhouses all over the west and I was never graduated from anything."

A NATION OF FANS

Laura responded to her new fans by writing *Farmer Boy. Farmer Boy* was about Almanzo's childhood on a farm in New York. It was published in 1933. After that, her publisher printed six more books as fast as Laura could write them.

Little House on the Prairie came in 1935, followed by *On the Banks of Plum Creek* in 1937. *By the Shores of Silver Lake* came out in 1939, *The Long Winter* in 1940 and *Little Town on the Prairie* the next year. She published her final book, *These Happy Golden Years,* in 1943. She wrote another book about her first years of married life, but it was not published until after her death.

In the middle of her writing, Laura and Almanzo traveled back to DeSmet for a visit. The town was very different from what Laura remembered. "Everywhere we went we recognized faces," she said. "We were always surprised to find them old and gray like ourselves instead of being young as in our memories."

That trip was to be the last time Laura saw her sisters. Grace died two years later in 1941 and Carrie five years after that. Tiny, silver-haired Laura was the sole survivor of her family. She grieved again in October 1949 when Almanzo died.

GOLDEN YEARS

Then as always, Laura found an inner strength. She had thousands of letters from adoring fans to cheer her. She was a popular author with libraries and awards named after her. Laura spent another seven years alone on Rocky Ridge Farm. She died on the farm just three days after her ninetieth birthday.

Laura's writing mirrored her life in many ways. Her books held happy endings. She wove a strong love of family through each, as well as a sense of determination and hard work. Many people were amazed she could remember so much from when she was so young.

"I have learned in this work that when I went as far back in my memory as I could and left my mind there awhile it would go back farther and still farther," she said once. "Also, to my surprise, I have discovered that I have led a very interesting life."

Laura Ingalls Wilder